The WiseWolf Job Search Pocket Book

How to Win Jobs and Influence Recruiters

Wendy Mason

First Published in Great Britain 2014
by Bluebird House Books
http://bluebirdhousebooks.com/

ISBN-13: 978-0992990008
ISBN-10: 0992990009

DEDICATION

This book is dedicated to all who have the courage to go out and learn the new skills necessary to find a job now. And of course to my wonderful editor, Beth, and my partner, Owen, who continues to provide support I appreciate more each day.

CONTENTS

ACKNOWLEDGMENTS

So many people along the way have provided ideas and inspiration. I have to mention my wonderful coaching clients; I continue to be grateful to them.

I am grateful as well to members of the Careers & Jobs (Open) CRE & Facilities Management LinkedIn Group and in particular Paul Carder (Doctoral Researcher & Tutor @UWEBristol; Founder, Occupiers Journal) who gave me the opportunity to manage the group and to Colin Sandler of EllisDon and Mark Southall of The FM Consultancy who provided their thoughts on what to include.

At the end of the day, any errors of omission or commission are entirely my own.

WENDY MASON

FOREWORD

This is pocket book for anyone looking for a job.

When I started my WiseWolf Talking blog (http://wisewolftalking.com/) in 2008, I hadn't got it in mind to write about job search. WiseWolf Talking started as a blog about leadership and management. But I couldn't ignore the changes I was seeing around me. More and more people were looking for help to find work.

As the recession bit, I saw people in all sectors being forced out of long-standing jobs. Most of them had expected to be employed for life. Many didn't have the basic tools needed to find a new job in the 21st century.

I saw many school leavers and graduates entering the job market ill-equipped to help themselves to find work.

One of my coaching clients left a leading public sector role without having ever had to produce a CV. When it came to job search, he told me he didn't have a clue where to start.

I was grateful for his honesty. This book is meant for him and others like him who have the courage to go out and learn the new skills necessary to find a job now.

WENDY MASON

INTRODUCTION

So you need to find a job. And I suppose, you have heard all kinds of stories about how difficult it is going to be. Well, yes, it is a challenge. But the truth is that lots of people are getting jobs right now and you can be one of them.

So what is it that marks out the successful job seeker?

Successful job hunting today takes commitment, confidence, flexibility, resilience and technique. And you'll find tips on all those things in what follows.

Commitment

You'll need to commit time and energy to your job search. Many successful job seekers spend 36 to 40 hours a week looking for work. Sounds just like work doesn't it? But keeping a regular routine and having structure pays great dividends.

Confidence

If you are not already a very confident person, or the experience that brings you here has knocked your confidence, the work we will do to help you understand and appreciate your past successes can help you to feel confident again.

Flexibility

Being willing to adapt and to accept change opens up all kinds of possibilities. This is certainly easier with more confidence. You'll explore flexibly meeting the needs of a potential employer in the pages that follow.

Resilience

Resilience, like confidence, is something you may have to work hard at. Finding work may take longer than you expect and you will probably have to bounce back from some knocks on the way. You will be in good company, though. Lots of good people have suffered the same kind of knocks only to bounce back and be very successful at their next attempt, or the one after that.

Technique

If you have been out of the job market for a while, there will be new techniques to learn and some you need to refresh. From writing a modern CV to wowing them at the interview, all the tips are here.

I advise my clients to treat job seeking as a full time occupation, if they can. This can be a challenge. Even if you don't need to take part-time work to generate money, the one at home is often expected to take more responsibility for covering the domestic chores; picking up the kids from school, etc. But successful job search requires a big investment of time.

If you are used to working conventional office hours then those are the hours I would recommend you commit to looking for work. Now is the time to set up a firm working routine and make a plan.

In broad terms you have four main tasks:

1. **Finding the right opportunities**

2. **Becoming the best candidate**

3. **Going through the recruitment process**

4. Making a good start in the new role.

Recognizing these tasks can help you to think through how to structure your time effectively.

You should spend part of each day:

➢ **Identifying new vacancies.** We'll talk more about this shortly.

➢ **Managing your networking campaign.** Identify possibilities, write letters, prepare to talk to people, make calls. (You could dedicate a particular day each week to meeting people to save on travel expenses).

➢ **Researching and learning.** Read everything you can get your hands on about job search in the current market and what recruiters are saying on sites like LinkedIn. Not all advice will be wise, nor will it all apply to you, but at least scan it for new tips. Research your sector thoroughly, learn about the very latest developments in your field, know the key players. If you have a vacancy in sight, thoroughly research the organization and their senior people. If you have some money to invest, spend it on updating your skills. If not, there are lots of free learning resources on-line.

➢ **Staying healthy and confident.** Take time each day to exercise and get fresh air. Work on recognizing your own competence and remembering your successes. These can be a great boost to your self-confidence.

Now let us start the real work on your job search!

WENDY MASON

FINDING THE RIGHT OPPORTUNITIES

WENDY MASON

What kind of work are you looking for?

Do you know the kind of work are you looking for?

The answer is going to be critical for success in your job search. But you may have some decisions to make before you are completely clear. The clearer you become about what you want, and the more you know about that kind of work, the simpler your job search becomes. And the more likely it is to be successful.

Now it is time to take up pen and paper and write down answers to the following questions.

Is this going to be a career move or simply finding a job to pay the bills?

You may be looking for work mainly so you can pay the bills to keep yourself and those you love. Or you may be focusing mainly on your career development building on skills and experience and looking for promotion opportunities. For most, it is a combination of the two and some people are simply looking for stop-gap work while they chase a career move. But, all may welcome a new challenge at work or a new environment. Where are you and where does the balance lie?

What do you really enjoy doing and what do you dislike?

We tend to work best at things we like. What do you

enjoy doing? Think about your interests and the things that you have enjoyed doing in the past in both your work and personal life. What kind of environment suits you best? Now look in the mirror and think honestly about what have you disliked doing and the environments you have disliked.

What are you good at?

Take some time to think about what you are really good at and your key skills? What do you bring to the party? We'll do more work on this when we write your STAR stories later.

What are you not so good at?

Remember nobody is good at everything. Taking a job that requires you to spend much of your time on things you are not good at, is full of risk. You are unlikely to succeed and you would be setting yourself up for stress.

Note: Taking a stop-gap role while looking for right opportunity may be a good idea. But if you hate the stop-gap work, it will sap the energy and motivation you need to find that real career opening.

How do you want to work?

It's important to decide how you want to work. Is this going to be a permanent, employed post or would you take on an interim role "temping" through agency or as an independent contractor? Could you take an internship or volunteer, which would give you experience but is likely to be unpaid. Think about traveling and commuting. How far away from home are you prepared to work? Are you prepared to move home? What about hours? Are you prepared for long days and working weekends?

What kind of organization do you want to work for?

Think about the variety of organizations that are around – large or small, public or private? What about working in a different sector, such as, finance, education or health? Each will have its own culture and opportunities.

How much do you need to earn?

When looking for a job, it is good to have an idea about money. You need to know, as well, how much money you need to get by. Then you need to know how much money you would like to earn. Work out a budget and be clear about the style of life you want to lead. How much money is it going to take to support you?

Now you have the answers to these questions, are you ready to begin your job search?

Not quite. What about your passion?

What is your passion?

Lots of people look for roles that reflect what they think they should want, not what they actually enjoy doing. And often they feel only half alive at work. If you feel passionately about what you do, it shows in the quality of your work and achieving is so much easier!

You need to understand what you really care about.

At interviews, you may well be asked about your passion. When you answer, you need to be practical. For example, saying that your passion is for something that is going to mean travelling to the other side of the world for weeks at a time may not get you that job with a local employer. Be honest. But think about what is going to present you in a reasonable light at your interview. And make sure that you can back up your statement with information about your past experience and future intentions. Do not declare a passion for something if you know very little about it.

Having and showing passion, and the energy associated with it, are attractive. Passion makes you more interesting to employers and to the world at large.

So, what is your passion?

What do you bring to the party?

STAR stories make you a star!

In searching for work, you will need to describe your achievements so far. This is so that you can demonstrate to a potential employer the real value that employing you will bring. Also, thinking about your achievements can be real boost to your self confidence. And you need lots of confidence to make your job search a success.

Writing STAR stories is a way to prepare not only to write your CV but also to answer questions at interview. This is particularly important for what are known as competency based interviews

How to write your STAR stories

The STAR method means that for each of your major achievements you will set out the:

- ★ **S – Situation.** Set out the background; when, where, who and why

- ★ **T – Task or tasks.** Be specific here. Explain exactly what you were required to do and what was the required outcome

- ★ **A – Action.** Describe what you did and what skills you used as well as how you behaved

- ★ **R – Result/Outcome** Describe what happened, the benefits and how you could measure them.

People like hearing a well-told story. Telling your STAR stories well will ensure you are memorable for the right reasons.

They should be

★ **Concise and pithy**

★ **Positive**

★ **Realistic**

You will not put all the detail from your STAR stories into your CV, but it really helps to have them around when, for example, you prepare for interviews. They will help to remind you of past successes.

Here is how to write your STAR stories

✓ Go right back to the beginning of your career.

✓ Use your laptop or simply get a notebook and note down all the good things you have achieved. We are talking here about your personal as well as career successes.

✓ Don't spend time on the things that you don't feel good about! But a whole program or initiative doesn't have to have been a success for your part of it to be something you are proud about.

✓ Now pick at least 10 achievements across your career. It will help you later if you include at least five from the more recent past. There is no limit though to the number of STAR stories you can produce.

✓ For each achievement, write a S.T.A.R story, setting out under each heading, Situation, Task, etc., what happened and clearly explaining your contribution.

✓ Of course you can write as much or as little as you like about each success. But at this stage about one page of A4 for each is usually sufficient.

✓ Start with your early achievements and work forward.

✓ Do your research if necessary about times, places and events. You are building a portfolio to be proud of, so make sure your stories are accurate.

✓ After you have completed each story take a pause and review. Enjoy your success. When you have completed five, lay them out before you and feel proud.

✓ When you are ready, type them up and print them out on good quality paper.

✓ Put them in a folder with your name on the front. You have begun your portfolio.

By the way, STAR stories don't have to be confined to paid employment. Have you had a voluntary role? Are there things you have done for your local community? Write the stories and put them in. They will all serve to show just what a valuable and competent person you are!

Bet you had forgotten that you are a STAR!

WENDY MASON

Where to look for work

There are a number of different places to look for work and your job search strategy will work best if you include all of them.

Working with recruitment agencies

Most job searchers sign up with one or more recruitment agencies. There are all kinds of agencies from large companies that operate nationally, and some internationally, across many sectors, to small niche agencies that specialize in particular sectors or particular geographical areas. It is a good idea to make contact with several. You can find lots of them on-line.

A good recruitment agency will keep you up-to-date with what is going on in the job market and help you prepare for any opportunity they offer you. Many agencies will have a mix of permanent and interim/contract roles. Register with the agencies with whom you feel comfortable. Make sure they are keeping you up to date with their vacancies.

Most recruitment agencies do a good job for employers and job seekers, but don't be naive. Don't forget that the employer is the real client. Nevertheless, it is in the agency's interest to help you succeed and you should expect courtesy and some support.

Be aware that, because so many people are looking for work, people without real expertise have set themselves up as recruiters. Even well qualified and experienced recruiters may be overwhelmed with numbers. Large agencies may mean less of a personal touch but small agencies can find themselves without the resources to cope with responses to popular jobs. Always ask lots of questions about what they offer and check friends and relatives for recommendations.

If you can, develop and maintain a real relationship with recruiters but recognize that pressures on them can lead to what appears to be an uncaring attitude. It is up to you help them to help you; nobody cares more than you do about your job search.

On-line job sites

On-line job sites give you immediate access to all kinds of jobs and you can search them in your own time at home. More and more employers are using sites like Manpower and Indeed to find new staff. You may find these sites provide lots of other resources to help you in your job search. Take time to browse and get a real feel for what is available. Before you search, think carefully about the keywords you will use to find possible jobs and use their user guides to make the most of the sites.

Newspapers and Magazines

Many national and local newspapers have adverts for jobs in both their printed papers and on their websites. Some specialize in particular sectors on particular days of the week.

Many national newspapers, for example, the Guardian in the UK, operate as on-line job sites and provide lots of resources for job seekers.

Local newspapers have always been a good source of information about local jobs and again they will have on-line sites. Local companies still advertise with local newspapers and use their online bulletin boards, so don't ignore them. Find out which day your local paper is published and, more importantly, which day they advertise jobs. Contact them and let them know the type of work you want, your skills and your experience. They may know of a suitable position or let you know if anything comes into the office.

Trade, sector specific and professional magazines usually carry job adverts and are a great source of information about networking and professional development opportunities.

Contacting employers directly

Most vacancies, particularly in the private sector, are never advertised. They are filled by people already known to the employer or known to a contact of the employer. So, of course, it is worthwhile making yourself known. There is no reason why you should not contact an employer to ask about available jobs. If an employer can fill a job without advertising, it saves them time and expense. Even if they don't have vacancies now and you make the right impression, they may contact you in the future.

Find out as much as you can about the organization before you approach them. Identify a suitable senior manager or professional and address your letter to them. Look for someone in a position of influence but outside HR. Then tailor your letter carefully to show your interest in the organization, tell them why you would like to work for them and how what you have to offer might meet their needs. Ask for an opportunity to talk to them to learn more about the organization and future opportunities. Offer to send your CV. Keep you letter simple, straight forward, polite and on one sheet. Check it very carefully for accuracy and typos.

Many people try to find out the name of person responsible for hiring new staff and write to them. But a direct approach to a senior executive in the department you want to work in is often more successful. If you have done your homework, and show a real interest in the company, you can find this direct contact can be a very good way in.

LinkedIn, Facebook and Twitter

Social networking is an incredibly powerful tool for the job seeker. LinkedIn, in particular, is a powerful business networking tool. It is used directly by employers to find staff as well as by head-hunters and recruitment agencies. Keep your own profile clean, up-to-date and professional.

Use social media and LinkedIn, in particular, to help you research organizations in your job search.

Follow the organizations you are interested in for possible recruitment activity as well as other news.

Make sure that your social activity doesn't weaken your opportunities, though. Remember everything you add will be out there for a prospective employer to find. Make social media work for you.

Graduate and intern schemes

If you are a recent university graduate (or about to become one) you should consider graduate schemes in your field of interest. They can be a fast track to the top but sometimes they have a high rate of attrition. Find out as much as you can about them before you commit. There will be information about how to apply on the organization's website.

They are usually very heavily subscribed so don't take it personally if you are not one of the very lucky few. But it is always worth giving it your best shot.

Internships are usually unpaid or very poorly paid. But they can provide valuable experience and a way into particular fields, for example, in the media. If you are young, don't have work experience and you can afford it, they are a good option. Again, you can research them on-line. You will find them on sites like Reed and Monster.

Voluntary work

Doing voluntary work while you are unemployed has lots of advantages so long as it leaves you time for your job search. As well as making you feel useful, it is usually a way to add to your portfolio of references and you may gain new skills. It can also be a useful source of opportunities. Don't hesitate to tell the contacts that you make while volunteering that you are looking for work.

Word of mouth – networking

Most jobs, particularly in the private sector, are never advertised at all. You can find out about those jobs through your friends and relatives and through networking. I'll cover networking later but for now just keep in mind that networking, for example, at conferences and exhibitions, can be a rich source of new contacts and opportunities.

Organize your job search

Be methodical in your approach. Make sure you keep track of who you have contacted or researched and the stage you've reached with each one. This means you will be able to follow up effectively and not duplicate your efforts.

Keep contact details on file with a system like Outlook. Maintain background files on the organizations you would like to work for and record the details carefully of opportunities that might interest you.

The best way to find work is by word of mouth networking.

THE WONDERFUL ART OF NETWORKING

WENDY MASON

Why you need to network

Everyone has a private network of friends and contacts. Work and professional networks are about building and maintaining relationships too. They are not about exploiting people.

In professional networking you are gathering information that may help you in your work not just your job search. But you should also be sharing information. You never know when you will need these relationships or when your contacts may need you and the information you provide.

Just like personal networks, professional networks are about reciprocal arrangements. And personal networks and professional networks blend into each other in terms of people offering mutual support.

Most jobs, certainly in the private sector, never get advertised. Many organizations prefer to hire someone known to be capable against the risk of an unknown "best" candidate. The degree of formality around filling these posts, even at quite senior level, varies widely.

This may come as something of a shock, particularly to former public sector employees where all posts are usually advertised.

Networking is critical in accessing this hidden market.

There is a huge amount to be gained from developing your contacts in terms of gathering industry and sector knowledge and hearing about these never-advertised positions.

A professional network is not just a nice-to-have; it's a must-have source of new work, support, advice, ideas and consolation. Strengthen relationships with people you already know and put some energy into meeting new people.

A small investment of time in networking can generate a large reward.

How to network to find a job

Job search networking is all about making connections with people. The people you want to contact are those who can either let you know about potential job openings or connect you with others who can.

Networking means talking to everyone you know

Everyone with whom you have regular contact can be part of your network. It doesn't matter if you don't know very many people. The people you do know might in turn know other people who have heard about a job opening.

Job search networking can be done at different levels

It can be a matter of having casual conversations with people you meet. Or you can make it an active and strategic campaign to contact people for ideas, suggestions and information.

Don't be afraid to ask for help

People are usually happy to help if they can. You have nothing to lose by phoning or meeting with your contacts. If you don't make the connection, you won't be able to tell if the person has good information or knows about an upcoming job. If you do speak with them, you might just land that job or hear about another that suits you better. At worst, you might feel a bit uncomfortable. But being prepared will make the discussions easier.

How to prepare For Job Search Networking

Make your list of all the people you know. Remember, they don't need to be friends, or even acquaintances; you just need to have enough of a common link with them to initiate a conversation. If you can pick up the phone and call them, for any reason, they are potential networking contacts.

Prepare what you are going to say. You don't want to just ring people up and say, 'I work in HR. Do you know of any jobs going?' Before you phone anyone, note down the specific details of what you're looking for and exactly the kind of help you think they might be able to give you.

You are now ready to network!

1. **Contact the people on your list in a systematic way.** Set yourself a goal. Maybe you're happy to spend all afternoon on the phone to people and cross twenty off your list. Or maybe you just want to work through the list steadily, making three calls a day. Always start the conversation inquiring about them and their well-being and make sure this is a convenient time to talk. If you find yourself losing enthusiasm, being less conversational and speaking more mechanically, it might be time to take a break.

2. **Don't be afraid to ask them for job leads.** Make it easy for them to help you. Ask them if they have any tips, leads or suggestions. Ask if they know of any vacancies for a person with your skills. If they don't, ask them to keep you in mind in case anything comes up.

3. **Most importantly, ask them if they can suggest anyone else you might contact**. Do they know someone else who might know about the kinds of jobs that you're after? Do they know anyone who works for this or that organization that you're interested in joining? If they can refer you to others, contact those other people and ask them the same questions.

4. **Follow up contacts.** Often people will tell you, 'I'll ask around and see what I can find out for you.' Sometimes they do ask around; sometimes they forget almost immediately or a crisis happens at work and they haven't the time. If you don't hear from them within a week or so, call them back to see if they've managed to find anything out.

5. **Stay polite.** Sometimes it seems as if no one will do anything for you or ask around on your behalf. It can be frustrating, but you should stay very polite and pleasant in your dealings with your contacts. After all, you're asking them for a favour.

6. **Follow up leads.** After your initial networking efforts and research, you'll probably have a long list of new people to try and make connections with. A phone call may be enough or you might want to arrange a meeting with them to introduce yourself and ask them more specific questions about their company or industry.

Keep networking. Even after you've found a job, keep networking. Networking isn't just for getting a job; it can help you do your job better, and it's a way of being part of your community and society.

The secret of networking is reciprocity. If there is something you can do for your contacts in return, make sure you do it. Never forget a favour done for you and if you can't return it to the person who did it, then make sure you do something for someone else.

If there is something you can do for your contacts in return, make sure you do it.

How to work a room

Whether you are looking for work or looking for promotion at work, knowing how to work a room is invaluable. You will find you are at lots of events where your ability to make contacts and get to know new people will be a major advantage.

Here are my top 10 tips for working a room.

1. **Find your crowd**. For career networking, go to every event where you are likely to meet people who might influence your future. Even in these days of virtual communication, personal contact makes all the difference. The more networking events, professional conferences, job fairs, professional associations, senior meetings, board meetings and other gatherings you go to, the better your chance of meeting someone who can help you. Getting into meetings and events with senior staff at work gets you noticed.

2. **Don't let lack of confidence be a barrier**. If nervous, go with a friend. Take a willing friend along. It can be much easier to have a conversation when you're not the only one trying to think of what to say. If you don't have someone to bring, then find the outlier on the edge of the crowd when you get there and start a conversation. Ask how they got there and who do they know. The chances are they are as nervous as you and will be grateful that you spoke to them. Don't be shy or embarrassed that you're unemployed. So are millions of other good people.

3. **Smile.** Smiles are contagious and they show energy. The more you smile, the more pleasant the

reception you'll get; people like people who smile. But make sure it is natural - remember the Cheshire Cat!

4. **Practice your introduction.** Prepare your short introduction or elevator speech (three lines about you and why you are there) before you get there and practice saying it.

5. **Keep the conversation going.** After you start a conversation by introducing yourself, keep up the momentum. It's much easier to converse when you're on first name terms with the person you are talking with – so exchange names. Then ask a question using their first name. Once you've said hello, ask the person you're talking to about their job or their field of interest. Show a genuine interest in them and what they are doing – people usually love talking about what they do. If you ask an open-ended question like "What do you think about..." you'll be able to keep the conversation rolling. Be a good listener and show you are interested in what they have to say. Listen more than you speak and don't interrupt their flow.

6. **Be prepared to answer questions.** If the person you're talking to seems interested in you and asks questions, answer them fully and don't be dismissive of what you have to offer. Be prepared to explain what qualifications and skills you have and what you are looking for. If you are in employment, be ready to talk about your job and make it interesting.

7. **Don't monopolize the conversation.** Spend time learning about others as well as talking about your goals but move on regularly. The more people you talk to, the more opportunities you'll have.

8. **Don't be negative.** People don't like negativity, so don't bad mouth your (old) job, your (old) boss and the company. Instead put a positive spin on your situation and your future plans.

9. **Give out your business cards.** Have business cards printed with your contact information (name, address, phone, email, LinkedIn profile, etc.) and be ready to hand them out. Never travel without them. A business card makes it easy for people to get in touch with you. Keep them in your pocket or the side of your bag so you can get to them without a lot of fuss.

10. **Accept their Business Cards.** and offer help if you can. If you're at a professional function, collect business cards. After the event, follow-up. Send a follow up email thanking the person for talking to you. Let them know you appreciate anything they can do to help. Offer to help with your contacts and information if you can. Perhaps send them an interesting article you have read or recommend a book. "Giving to get" works every time. Offering to help someone else with their career goals or with job leads will pay you back with more help than you might imagine.

Be a good listener and show you are interested in what they have to say.

Networking on-line and with social media

Back in the day, you painstakingly typed out one CV and posted that to all potential employers. The next generation attached that same one CV to an email and sent it out. Then we learned to turn one electronic CV into several to meet the needs of a particular job and a particular employer.

Now, things have moved on again. Your CV has become an active, living part of your job search. It is very much tied into how you present yourself on-line and your personal "brand."

Most employers now research on-line all candidates for significant appointments. They will put your name into a search engine like Google and see what comes up. And they will expect to find you. This may come as a shock to many older employees where having a low public profile has usually been regarded as an asset.

In fact, the chance that they will find nothing about you on-line is becoming more and more remote.

Having nothing about you on-line is a clear disadvantage in job search. It sends a message that you wouldn't feel comfortable with modern office tools.

So, rather than leave it to chance, you need to know what is on-line about you and take steps to influence it for the good.

There are huge advantages in using social media in your job search anyway. Using sites like Twitter,

Facebook and, particularly, LinkedIn is a great way to network, to find new opportunities and to raise your on-line profile.

Make sure you have a well filled out LinkedIn profile. There is lots of advice on the site for how to do this. Fill it out completely using keywords – the words people will use to find someone who does your type of work. Putting in those keywords won't just help people find you on LinkedIn, they could also help you rank higher up in Google when someone does a general search for your name.

You need to check what else is on-line about you already. Put your own name into Google and see what comes up. If there is something unhelpful, where you can, do your best to put things right. For example, if there is an unflattering picture of you on Facebook, ask the person who put it there to remove it. There is a lesson here for the future in terms of what you put on-line yourself or allow others to post. These days, I try to avoid anyone taking pictures of me with their phone at parties and events.

Be careful in future how you use social media. Remember that your tweet on twitter or your comment on Facebook lives on forever.

Have a particular care on Facebook – learn about the security settings and check for changes regularly. Remember that what you treat as private may not be treated in the same way by "friends."

If you blog, be aware that your post will live on to be read by potential employers.

Never, never record on-line your inner most and negative thoughts about your employer or those you have worked with. Do not make jokes about them either.

Overall, you need to integrate the social media approach to job searching with the traditional approach you've used in the past. Be consistent, be positive and don't let there be any surprises on-line for recruiters.

Make sure what the potential employer sees in the application form lines up with what they find on-line.

WENDY MASON

BECOMING THE BEST CANDIDATE

That winning CV

You'd be surprised how many people have never had to write a CV.

It can be a daunting task. So, here is some help.

'CV' stands for 'Curriculum Vitae' which means 'story of your life.' But, in this context, it means a brief written account of your career so far. The intention is to sum up all the basic information that an employer needs to know in one short and easy-to-read document. A CV is comparable to a résumé in many countries; in French, résumé means summary.

Your CV is a great way of showing a potential employer just what value they will get when they employ you. It is the most valuable product in your job search tool kit and it is more than just a list of roles.

Once you have written a basic CV, you could then simply send that document to many employers. But it is important to adapt this basic template to meet the needs of any particular job advert and the organization you wish to join.

You can send a copy of your CV when you're applying for a specific job vacancy or when you're just writing to enquire about possibilities.

At its most basic, a CV is just a short list of facts about you and your work history, skills, qualifications and experience. A good CV is essential when looking for work and it is worth spending time getting it right so that it really markets you to an employer.

So what will an employer be looking for?

Your CV should show

> ➤ **Contact details:** name, address, post code, telephone number, e-mail and Skype address

> ➤ **Headline and Profile:** a short summary

> ➤ **Keywords;** words to attract recruiters

> ➤ **Competencies:** skills and personal qualities

> ➤ **Experience:** employment history and other experience demonstrating your competencies

> ➤ **Qualifications:** formal qualifications, professional memberships and awards

> ➤ **Education:** including training and academic achievements

> ➤ **Special skills:** keep to those appropriate e.g. driving licence

> ➤ **Interests:** if directly relevant to the job or organization.

The order may vary depending on the opportunity for which you are applying.

There are different 'styles' of CV

A modern CV is more likely to be required now. It starts with a pen picture of yourself which highlights your skills and experience relevant to the job. It then sets out the last five years (sometimes ten years) of job history emphasizing competence and achievements. Earlier work history and education, unless directly relevant to the work, are provided in a very short summary after that and sometimes left out entirely.

A 'traditional' CV lists everything in date order starting with your education and qualifications, followed by your employment history, interests etc. Traditional CVs are more likely to be required for academic institutions.

Variations and combinations of the two approaches may be required, determined by what it takes to demonstrate that you are the right person for this particular job or organization.

Your CV is a great way of showing a potential employer just what value you bring.

WENDY MASON

Writing a winning CV that stands out from the crowd

Any CV that you write is only relevant if it shows how you meet the requirements of a particular role. So you need to be ready to tailor you generic CV for each post.

Be specific about skills, experience and personal qualities. Show that you understand their requirements.

These days, employers and recruiters receive sacks full of CVs. Make yours short (no more than two sides of A4), easy to read and attractive. Lay it out clearly with enough space and clear section headings.

Your CV shows what you bring to the organization, so make it look professional. Choose a clear, professional font that is easy to read (e.g. Arial, Calibri, Times New Roman.) Check for typos; CVs with typos get "binned". A simple spell check is not enough; ask someone else to proof-read your finished CV.

Don't go for complicated designs with tables and fancy fonts. Use a simple, clean format that is well organized and easily scanned. That will attract both the recruiter's eye and, these days often more importantly, it is easy for the recruiter's software to process.

Have clear headings (work experience, education, etc.) so that these can be scanned quickly. Order your experience and education into reverse chronological order with the latest first. For recent posts, sum up what you actually achieved and delivered for each post. In these hard economic times, if you have saved an organization money or generated new business, make sure you flag that with figures and facts.

Keywords are important

Many recruiters use software to search candidates' CVs for specific keywords. It is important to include those which are likely to apply to the particular job.

Create clear statements that demonstrate your skills and show what you deliver, using terms that show you as positive and pro-active.

Keep away from buzzwords at all costs; for example "effective."

Make sure the keywords you use will resonate with the recruiter and the organization you wish to join. They should reflect skills and experience the employer is looking for in the recruit.

Go through these steps to find the best keywords.

➡ **Read the job advert** carefully. Make sure you understand exactly what the employer is looking for

➡ **Pick out keywords** from the advert and job spec that reflect the requirement

➡ **Sprinkle those keywords** across your CV, making sure you can back up what you claim.

The key to your keywords is to sprinkle them lightly. If you cram them in, it will look as if you copied and pasted from the advert and your CV will lack credibility. It will be headed for the bin.

Start your CV with contact details, a headline and a short summary profile

Follow clear contact details including name, address, email and telephone numbers with a one line headline that describes you. Check out the professional headlines on LinkedIn for models; for example:

"Expert program manager with experience of mission critical programs."

Make this kind of headline your model. Then follow up with a short profile that sums up your skills and experience.

If you are just starting out, your profile can include your career goals.

Your profile is a part of your CV that you should certainly tailor to the particular needs of the specific job for which you are applying. These are words that will flag up to a recruiter why you are right for the role. Some recruiters will not read much further.

Essentially, a profile is a very condensed and targeted version of a covering letter. And there are clear benefits to including a good one. It can help you stand out among the hundreds of applications that companies receive.

Most employers spend only a few seconds looking at your CV and most of this time is spent looking at the top half. So, even if a potential employer reads only your profile (located directly beneath your name and contact information), they will still have a clear idea of how uniquely well-fitted you are for the role.

Keep your profile concise; between one and four short sentences and you can use bullet points. Focus on the requirements for the job and what you have to offer.

Overall, relate your employment history and skills to the requirements listed for the job. Make sure that, at first glance, you look the best candidate.

How do you begin to put your career history on paper?

You want to show a successful career progression that makes the next opportunity (the one you have just decided to apply for) look like a logical move. Making it look like a natural fit can put you ahead in the job market. It marks you out as the candidate they want.

Start with the latest and focus on the last five to ten years. Sum up your earlier career history. If there are gaps in your employment history, be prepared to explain them and show what you gained from the experience.

For your three latest jobs, show your employer and the role you held, with dates. Then, for each, describe briefly what you achieved in the job to demonstrate that you have competencies for the role for which you are applying.

Produce a baseline CV and then adapt it to each job or organization that you apply for. That way, you can target your qualifications, skills, and key strengths with relevant keywords. You want to appeal to the person advertising the job at first glance.

A CV that is going to win you the job is the one that makes the reader want to know more about you.

Completing an application form and covering letter

You should regard your covering letter and CV as an opportunity to sell yourself to employers. They are going to be reading your covering letter before your CV so it's important that it makes an impact.

Covering letters that create a good first impression are well constructed, contain no spelling mistakes and support what you are saying in your CV.

A good letter should capture the recruiter's attention and make them want to read your CV. It should show you have done your research. This means showing you understand what the job involves and what the employer wants. Your letter will need to convince an employer that you are really interested, you want the job and you are the best person for it.

The tone of a good covering letter should be confident but not arrogant.

Your covering letter should have a start that grabs the reader's attention. A middle that shows why you're the best person for the job. And a finish that pulls it all together and leads naturally on to what is happening next.

Your letter should not be longer than one page but it should show why you want to work for the organization and what skills and experience you can bring to the job. You need to research both the job and the organization thoroughly before you put pen to paper.

You don't need a covering letter if there is a section on an application form where you can provide additional information such as why you want to work for them. If there isn't an additional information section, include a covering letter, if you can, showing why you want to work for the organization and why you are right for the job.

Application forms

If the form is on-line, draft your application offline first in a word processing package like Word and save it to your computer. That way you'll be able to run a spell check before you copy the information into the on-line system. It means, as well, that you'll have a back-up if there's a problem with the form.

If you're filling in a form by hand, write as neatly as you can in black ink. Make sure you use block capital letters if the form asks you to.

If the employer has requested a completed application form, that's what they want. Don't be tempted to send back an incomplete application form with your CV attached.

It's a good idea to be positive about your reasons for leaving jobs, no matter how you feel about employers past or present.

Keep your answers short - you'll normally have just a small space next to each job in the work history section.

When you've written one application showing your skills, experience and strengths, use it as a template. Keep it so that you can cut and paste if appropriate for other applications. Always make sure though that you don't mention the wrong employer or job.

On-line application systems vary so follow instructions carefully. The form should include instructions and will usually have a section like this:

'please use this section to explain why you feel you are suited to this job and what you can bring to it'

or

'please include any further information relevant to the person specification, such as which skills, knowledge and experience you have'.

The employer will have seen which qualifications and work experience you have in the previous sections on the form. So the purpose of this section is for you to show you're motivated to do the job and that you have carefully considered why you feel you would be good at it.

If you claim any skill, remember to include an example to show how you have used it in the past. Set out what you say clearly in a way that is easy to read.

Even if you haven't got exactly the experience asked for, you could show how you have similar experiences and skills that would help you approach this opportunity.

You need to show your enthusiasm for the job and what attracted you to the organization. Try to use very positive language to describe what you could bring to the company.

It will impress employers if you show some knowledge of the organization, such as what they do, their strengths and any latest development that might have been in the news.

Set out what you say clearly, make sure it is easy to read and check carefully before pressing send.

Providing recruiters with your references

Recruiters usually ask for references when you apply for a job. But many job seekers feel uncomfortable about approaching potential referees. You shouldn't feel embarrassed though. Most people feel flattered when asked, however, you should give them the opportunity to say no. Tell them you will understand if they feel they simply don't know you well enough to help.

Here are my top tips for providing recruiters with your references.

- ✓ **Don't add referees to your CV.** When providing references, list them on a separate page or piece of paper.

- ✓ **Provide at least three.** If the recruiter doesn't specify how many are required, provide three with clear contact information. Contact details should include name, role, organization, postal address, email and telephone number.

- ✓ **Who to choose?** Include professional connections who will say things that support how well you are qualified for the job. You could include employers, colleagues and customers from previous jobs. Also people you have worked with as a volunteer or studied with like teachers and lecturers.

✓ **Short on professional references?** Include a personal reference who can attest to your character and abilities.

✓ **Your present employer.** If your present employer doesn't know you are applying, don't provide their name at an early stage. If you are successful you may be asked to provide their details later. Have care when you tell your present employer you are applying elsewhere and show them how you aim to support your current work before any move.

✓ **Ask permission.** Always ask permission before you give someone's name and tell them about any vacancy where you have mentioned them.

✓ **Remind your referees how good you are.** I usually suggest people explain the vacancy to their referees and remind them why they think it is a good fit.

✓ **Are you in the public sector?** Many public sector organizations will only offer bland references as your employer. When it arrives their reference may only be a statement that you worked for them in a particular grade or role over a particular period of time. Most large private sector employers know this but for others you may have to explain. You will usually need something more. Try asking your line manager or someone in your management line if they would be prepared to give you a personal reference as well as the one sent officially by HR. Many managers are more ready than you expect to help. Also consider approaching retired senior colleagues and others who have left the organization. You might also consider asking for a personal reference from someone who holds a senior position in the private sector. This is where people you have met during work in a voluntary capacity may be useful. Otherwise, consider people you have met through clubs and associations.

✓ **Say thank you.** It is courteous to thank your referees and let them know the outcome of your application. Who knows, if you are unsuccessful, they may be only too happy to let you know about a vacancy they have just heard about.

Most people feel flattered when asked to give a reference.

WENDY MASON

Preparing for the interview

Some employers like to go straight from application to the interview stage. Others screen candidates by asking them to take tests or to attend an assessment centre. Sometimes, they like to have a telephone discussion before inviting you to a face to face interview. We'll cover assessment centres and telephone interviews later but let's start with conventional job interviews.

Preparing for your interview is incredibly important. This is what can make you successful. You would be surprised how many people do not take the time to prepare properly. Preparing means you begin to understand the organization you are applying to join and it helps build your confidence.

Here is how to prepare

➢ **Research the organization.** Interviewers today expect you to know what the company does in some detail, particularly the part of the organization you wish to join. You need to understand how it is structured and the sector it operates in, as well as the main competitors. You can use the Internet to find out who are the key players in the organization. LinkedIn is a great tool for this.

➢ **Research the role.** Make sure you understand the job description thoroughly and how the role fits into the organization. Understand what skills they are looking for and think through examples you can use to show that you have them.

> **Research the interview**. The idea is to be as well prepared as possible and to have as few surprises on the day as possible. Make sure you understand what kind of interview you are going for and how it will be carried out. Don't be worried about asking about this – it shows real commitment to the process.

> Find out if there will be any tests or exercises on the day and whether they expect you to prepare a presentation. Is there anything they would like you to bring with you? Enquire about the interviewers themselves – who are they and what role do they hold in the organization?

> Make a list of points that you want the panel to know about you, for example, key successes in your previous role. If you can, and it is relevant, include the information in the answers you give at the interview. If you don't get the opportunity to give the information in answers then you will probably get an opportunity to add it at the end as "anything else".

Preparing means you understand the organization you are applying to join and it helps you build confidence.

Dress for success

It is said that over 50% of another person's perception of you is based on how you look. So, yes, of course it makes a difference what you wear to the interview.

Like so many other things you do to get work, dressing right needs research and preparation. You need to research the organization you are hoping to join for how employees dress.

In general, it is best to dress conservatively. In some organizations, for example in the Arts, that means smart casual. And smart casual means what it says, smart. Generally for interviews go for the mainstream.

For most organizations, what will be required will be smart office wear; a suit in one dark colour with a coordinated blouse or shirt in a light colour, white if you can wear it.

As for shoes, for women keep to a dark court shoe with a moderate heel and for men go for dark socks and professional shoes. All well-cleaned of course. Ties with logos are best avoided; again be reserved.

Go for a limited amount of jewellery and neat, clean hair. Nails need to be clean and manicured. Go lightly with the scent/aftershave. If someone on the panel starts to sneeze, they will not be concentrating on you and what you offer.

You want the panel to concentrate on you and on what you are saying, not on how you have dressed.

It should go without saying that your clothes should be clean and freshly pressed. If you have to travel a long way to get to the interview then consider using a suit bag and changing nearby.

If you do need to eat and drink in your interview clothes before the interview then do so with care and make sure crumbs are brushed off.

If possible, leave travel bags outside the interview room. If you carry anything into the room, it is best for it to be a portfolio or a brief case. Make sure you can get access to a clean tissue just in case your nose starts to run with all the tension.

Just like most other things you do to get a job, dressing for the interview is about research and preparation. But dressing well and appropriately really will help keep up your confidence on the day and it will certainly help you make your best impression.

Generally for interviews, dress for the mainstream.

What happens at the interview and how to answer questions

Most interviews follow a pattern. After welcoming you and making introductions, the interviewers will usually:

> **Tell you about the organization** and the role

> **Ask you questions** so that they can assess your abilities, your personality and your motivation

> **Encourage you to ask questions** about the job, the organization or the process

> **Tell you about the next stage** of the process and when a final decision will be made.

Remember that the interview is a two-way process. You're there to find out information about them as much as they are there to find out about you. So take your chance to find out information that isn't in the job description; this can help you make an informed decision about whether you definitely want the job.

How to answer questions

First, remember to keep a balanced approach. However strongly you feel about an issue, stay cool at the interview but not too detached. Show warmth, enthusiasm and commitment but never anger or despair.

The panel want you to succeed. There is nothing recruiters like better than to have the candidates they select for interview do well.

You will probably be asked a range of different kinds of questions. Some may be simple to answer and others much more challenging. Tough questions are not asked to make you feel uncomfortable but they are meant to test you.

Sometimes, you may be put under pressure just to see how well you cope with stressful situations. If you have applied for a high pressure job then you should expect this! Stay calm and show them how well you would cope.

Many interviewers start the interview with "getting to know you" factual questions about your experience. These are usually intended to put you at your ease and help you give your best. You may well be asked why you applied for the role and you need to prepare a credible answer. It should show you have some real interest in the organization and in the role.

You may well be asked why the organization should hire you. This is your opportunity to set out your wares. Again prepare for this. You should make sure your answer is compatible with your application form. It is often wise to check your application form just before the interview to make sure you keep your answers consistent.

You will probably be asked why you left your last position. Be honest but have a care. It is never wise to be critical of a previous employer. The same thing applies if you are asked to describe your worst boss. Give a balanced view. Show how you have learned from the experience!

If you are asked about your weaknesses, be honest and be brief but don't be trite. Concentrate on a minor shortcoming that doesn't have a profound effect on job performance. For example, you might mention a tendency, in your enthusiasm, to over-commit and take on too much work. But then you would go on to explain that you've learned to pace yourself. *(Please see the section following;* **The three most common interview questions.***)*

If the role has a management or leadership element, you may be asked for an example of something you handled well. Have some challenging examples ready to quote.

If you are asked what you are looking for in a role, have an answer ready that shows a real taste for the work and some enthusiasm.

If you are asked what you are looking for financially, ask what the salary range is for the position. But be ready in case you aren't given the information you need. Read salary surveys, government data and association reports in advance so you have an idea of what comparable jobs pay right now. That way, you can give a response that's in line with current standards.

Remember in all your answers to treat the panel with respect. Stay calm, be polite and do not patronize them. Whatever questions they ask, stay away from politics and religion in your answers!

When they are asking questions, listen carefully and take a deep breath before answering. Think before your speak. If there is something you don't understand, then ask for clarification. It may feel that, when thinking, you have left a long silence before you answer. What feels long to you will only really be seconds for the interviewers.

At the end of the interview, you will probably be asked if you have any questions. These days you are expected to say yes. Have something prepared about the role and how it might develop. Again, show a real interest in this role, these people and this organization.

The three most common interview questions

Although there is no set format that every job interview will follow, there are some questions that you can almost guarantee will crop up. Here are the three most common questions and a guide to the kind of answers your interviewer wants to hear.

Tell me about yourself

This is often the opening question and, as first impressions are key, one of the most important. Keep your answer to under five minutes, beginning with an overview of your highest qualification then running through the jobs you've held so far in your career.

You can follow the same structure as your CV, giving examples of achievements and the skills you've picked up along the way.

Don't go into too much detail. Your interviewer will probably take notes and ask for you to expand on any areas where they'd like more information.

If you're interviewing for your first job since leaving education, focus on the areas of your studies you most enjoyed and how that has led to you wanting this particular role.

What are your weaknesses?

The dreaded question! It is best handled by picking something that you have made positive steps to redress. For example, if your IT ability is not at the level it could be, state it as a weakness but then tell the interviewer about training courses or time spent outside work hours to improve your skills. That way your initiative could be perceived as a strength.

On no account say: "I don't have any weaknesses". Your interviewer won't believe you. Don't say: "I have a tendency to work too hard." That is usually seen as avoiding the question.

What are your strengths?

Pick the three attributes that you think most likely to get you the job and give examples of how you have used these strengths in a work situation. They could be tangible skills, such as proficiency in a particular computer language, or intangible skills, such as good management.

If you're not sure where to start, prepare by taking a look at the job description. There is usually a section listing candidate requirements. That should give you an idea of what they are looking for.

Above all, remember that the interviewers will be willing you on to do well.

WENDY MASON

Getting on with the interview panel

A number of different people can be involved in the interviewing process. They may be from different parts of the organization with an interest in the role who can give a range of perspectives. Sometimes, outside HR consultants are invited in to help the panel or someone from the recruitment company.

Job interviews conducted by a panel are seen to be fair and valid because a number of different opinions and views are taken into account in making a decision.

It can sometimes be difficult to build rapport with all panel members during the interview.

There may be one panel member that you find it particularly difficult to get on with. This can happen at an interview, just as it can in other parts of your life.

Here are some tips to help you build rapport with the interviewing panel

1. Knowing who the panel members are beforehand is a great help. If you can, research people on the Internet using LinkedIn, for example. If this is not possible, use your knowledge of the company and the position to prepare to respond to questions from different parts of the organization like human resources, line management, technical and finance.

2. Your introduction is important to creating the right first impression. This is a good opportunity to connect with each panel member on a personal level before the interview questions begin. Make initial eye contact with each panel member and try to respond warmly and with interest.

3. When the questions start, listen carefully to what is being asked and don't be afraid to ask for clarification or to make sure you understand correctly. It is important to answer the question that has been asked.

4. Make initial eye contact with the person who asked the question and then include the other panel members in your answer. Scan from one face to the next, pausing briefly on each. Focus on speaking to each individual and then, as you finish your answer, return your focus to the person who asked the interview question. Stay calm and answer each question thoroughly.

5. If you do get into a discussion or you are asked to consider an alternative point of view, again, stay calm. Do not expect to be successful if you let anger or annoyance show. Take time to respond with a considered view. Watch your body language, you can show frustration without saying a word.

A word of caution

Is there someone on the panel with whom you really cannot get on? Don't ignore how they make you feel and why.

If that person is to be your immediate boss in the new organization, or someone further up the line to whom you will report, think very carefully whether the role is right for you. Do this even if you are successful and it is a generous offer. I have worked with a number of clients who sensed at interview that all was not well but ignored those feelings, only to have regrets later.

With the right preparation and approach you should get on well with all the members of the interview panel.

Behavioural or competency based interview?

Behavioural or competency based interviewing is a style of interviewing that more and more organizations are using in their hiring process. This is based on a belief that the most accurate predictor of future success is past performance in a similar situation. So this form of interviewing is based on your experiences, the way you behave and your knowledge, skills and abilities.

Traditional interviewing includes general questions such as "Tell me about yourself." Behavioural interviewing is much more probing.

How do behavioural or competency based interviews work?

Employers prepare for this kind of interviewing by deciding the skills they think are necessary for the job. They then ask questions to find out if you have those skills.

For example, if leadership is necessary for a role, you may be asked to talk about an experience you have had as a leader and what you think makes a good leader.

In any interview, you should always listen carefully to the question. Don't be afraid to ask for clarification if you don't understand something. It is better to do this than to jump in uncertain of what is needed.

How to prepare for a behavioural or competency based interview

When going for any interview, you should research the organization carefully. You should also look at similar jobs in the same sector.

You are trying to find the qualities required.

Remember to note any qualities they mention in the advert or in the information pack. Then find useful examples of your demonstration of those qualities from your past and your CV/resume. Look for times when you have demonstrated the behaviours you think the organization is seeking.

During the interview:

➢ **Be specific.** Your responses need to be specific and detailed.

➢ **Be focussed.** Tell them about a particular situation that relates to the question, not a general one.

➢ **Be clear.** Outline the situation, what you did specifically and the positive results that followed.

➢ **Make it personal.** Be certain to show clearly what you contributed and how you did it.

This form of interviewing is based on your experiences, the way you behave and your knowledge, skills and abilities.

Assessment centres, phone interviews and group interviews

Assessment centres and tests

If you're expected to sit numerical reasoning and psychometric tests before an interview or during assessment days, you need to prepare.

Ask as much as you can about the process and if past examples are available.

The techniques do vary but there is plenty of information on-line. Also, there are many companies offering free on-line tests. This means you can see how well you do and the areas you need to improve if you are to get the job you want.

Here are my top tips for handling Assessment Centres

1. **Be Yourself!** Work on the basis the assessors know what they are doing. They will be able to see through an act. Keep your wits about you and show your best but try to relax enough to let the real you shine through. You may want to use a simple relaxed breathing technique during the odd break.

2. **Know the criteria.** Usually, the assessors will be assessing you against a predefined list of qualities and competencies for the job. For most public sector jobs you'll probably know what these are before the event. In the private sector, openness can vary. But you should try to find out the criteria before the assessment

centre. If you applied through a recruitment agency, they should be able to help. At the very least, the job description will usually give you an indication of the qualities they are looking for.

3. **Manage your time carefully.** Many candidates at assessment centres fail to do themselves justice because they run out of time in the exercises. Where you have to read a brief and then do an exercise afterwards, start by skim reading to get an idea of the issues. Then go back and study important points more carefully. Keep an eye on your watch and allocate your time carefully.

4. **Don't put other candidates down.** Remember, at an assessment centre you are unlikely to be measured directly against each other. You are being measured against the criteria for the role. Scoring points off others in group exercises doesn't make you look good. It makes you look like a non-team player and that is not likely to make the assessors warm to you. Your best strategy is usually to support, not to compete.

5. **Practice if you can.** It really helps if you can run through possible exercises with someone you trust as preparation for the centre. You will find organizations that offer paid-for practice online.

6. **Listen carefully to all instructions.** Know what you are doing and show you are doing it. Listen carefully to all instructions and show you are listening through your body language.

7. **Interact with the assessors.** If there is an opportunity to interact with the assessors, say at lunch time, then make the most of it. But don't be a nuisance and certainly don't hog the limelight. You want to make an impression memorable for the right reasons.

This book is helpful "Succeeding at Assessment Centres For Dummies".

The phone or Skype interview

Preparing for a phone interview

Lots of organizations now use phone or Skype interviews to screen candidates. This helps them cut costs and narrows the pool of applicants.

You need to take phone interviews seriously – you don't want to lose out to better prepared candidates.

A telephone interview is as important as any other form of interview or recruitment process. The first impression you make on the phone, how you present yourself, answer questions and handle the conversation, will decide whether you go forward.

As for a face-to-face interview, you need to find out as much as you can about the organization and the job. The best place to start is the employer's website. This will give you the background information you need, the size and structure of the organization, what it does and the field/market it works in.

Carry out a quick on-line search for news about the organization, such as, is it planning to expand or is it in difficulties? Referring to this with positive ideas can help you to stand out, particularly if you have possible solutions to problems. You can certainly show familiarity with the issues they are currently addressing.

Before the interview, prepare any questions you want to ask about the role, their culture and opportunities for growth in the company.

Make sure you have a pen and paper handy for note taking and have your CV to hand. They will probably open with questions about your experience.

And, odd as it may sound, dressing as you would for an interview to handle the call usually helps you to sound more professional.

Make sure you will not be interrupted and that you are settled and in a comfortable position to answer the phone before they ring.

If you are using Skype, dress as for an interview and check the background. A plain wall is preferable to an untidy room or office. Make sure the technology is working properly before the call. It is a great idea to practice with a friend beforehand.

Group interviews

Some organizations invite several candidates to attend an interview together. If you are invited for a group interview, again prepare by finding out about the organization and the job.

The advantages that group interviews provide for the employer is that they can see you both as a team player and as a leader. If you are given a topic to discuss, it can be an opportunity to show both capabilities. You can give a well argued opinion and lead the discussion. But you should also spend time listening carefully to what others say and taking forward the discussion with them.

You can ask questions for clarity and at some stage you can sum up the discussion. Don't try to put others down, show you can lead the group into a useful discussion where everyone takes part. That is most likely to get you an invitation to the next stage.

Assessment centres, phone interviews and group interviews require, above everything, very good preparation.

AFTER THE INTERVIEW

When the interview goes wrong

You can put lots of effort into preparing for an interview but still, sometimes, just sometimes, something goes wrong. You know when it happens and you suspect the interviewing panel know it too!

Perhaps you woke up not feeling well or something had happened in your private life to distract you. Maybe something happened on the journey. Whatever it was, something threw you off your best performance. And now you feel bad about it.

Can you get a second chance?

Well, here is the good news!

Although not all, there are many employers who may be willing a give you the benefit of the doubt if you are well fitted in other ways. Going back quickly, thanking them for the time they have spent on you already and explaining your circumstances may just do the trick.

> ➢ Don't go over the top but email or write to them briefly explaining what went wrong.

> ➢ Make sure you emphasize your interest in the job and ask if it is possible to meet a second time or perhaps arrange a phone interview.

> ➢ Remind them of your referees and that they will be willing to confirm what a good candidate you are.

> ➤ Set out again briefly why you really want this job and your interest in working for the organization. Then sum up why you are particularly well fitted for the role.

Don't forget to remind them again of your contact details.

You have nothing to lose by going back to them.

Say thank you

Saying thank you after the interview is a must

You can do it by email or by letter but you can't avoid it. It has become so much of a custom that some employers think less of you these days if you don't do it.

Send your thanks within 24 hours of being interviewed, if you can, and you need to tailor your letter it to suit the organization. The style should reflect the kind of organization and the type of interview you've had. A formal process requires a formal response.

If you are not sure what to write, then you can use a thank you letter template as a guide. You'll find lots of them on-line.

Your letter is a chance to emphasize what a good fit you are for the job now that you know more about it.

Even if you have decided the organization is not one you want to join, still send polite thanks. Who knows what the future holds? And you might have made some useful contacts.

This is a good opportunity to flag up things they need to know but didn't ask at the interview. You can add what you didn't mention or make something clearer.

If you have some information that might be useful to them or thoughts on helping them solve an issue they raised, it can help you to stand out from the crowd.

Some people recommend writing to everyone you spoke to in the organization. But I would usually write only to the person who is leading job search within the organization.

Remember to proof-read your letter carefully; nothing is more off-putting than reading a letter from a candidate that includes typos. If you are not sure of the spelling of names and the correct titles, then ring the organization to check.

Remember, timing comes before creative brilliance. Get your letter in as soon as you can - most organizations make their minds up about interviewees pretty quickly.

You can do it by email or by letter but you can't avoid it. Say thank you!

Negotiating a remuneration package

So you did well at interview and you are now being offered the role. But what about the remuneration package? Should you accept what they are offering?

Here are some things to consider:

> **What can you afford to accept?** You need to understand all your financial commitments and what it takes to maintain your present life style.

> **What are you earning now?** Surely you would expect at least the same salary.

> **What is the market rate for the job** and what are other people being paid for the same work? Find job specs with similar requirements to what you've been offered and check what other employers are currently offering. If you are particularly well qualified or experienced, you should expect higher than average market rates.

Now work out your ideal salary. This is the salary you consider you should be paid, given the job you're applying for and your own level of experience. Look at the higher-end salaries for jobs being advertised in your chosen field, as well as the level of experience they require.

Your prospective employer might offer any of the following benefits:

- ✓ Health care
- ✓ Pension scheme
- ✓ Stock options
- ✓ Free gym membership
- ✓ Travel schemes/car
- ✓ Flexible working options
- ✓ Training opportunities
- ✓ Professional memberships

Consider how much flexibility you're willing to offer in return for these kind of benefits. That means considering the monetary value of each benefit as well as the effect on your life style. For example, flexible working hours might allow you to spend more time with your family and pensions could help your future security.

Now, you have a fair idea what you might expect and it is time to think about negotiating.

Your new employer is likely to have a figure in mind for your salary, but think twice about simply accepting or rejecting the first offer. See how much flexibility there is and when a salary review is likely to take place. This might make taking a slightly lower offer more acceptable.

If it is a low offer, tell the new employer that is what you think. Tell them tactfully and back it up with facts from your research.

If the package is around your expected salary, you can still try to negotiate. Explain how your experience, knowledge and qualifications position you in the market. If you are one of those lucky people offered your ideal salary, you can still discuss future opportunities for earning and for career development.

Never just refuse the offer of a salary straight away. Always say you 'need time to consider the package', that gives you and the employer more time to think about your options.

Never consider salary in isolation. Always take into account other things in the package and make sure you understand them.

Do consider the work culture and the nature of the job itself as well as career development opportunities when making your decision. And keep a long term perspective; where is taking this job likely to lead?

If the salary is not what you expected and it isn't compensated for by additional benefits or career development, you should say so. If the employer is not prepared to move, then you may have to accept the job wasn't right for you and move on. But do that with care.

If you've done your homework, you should know what you're worth, so you should try your best to make sure that's what you earn in your next job.

When you have considered salaries, you should consider the possible benefits package.

WENDY MASON

So you didn't get the job

First, don't take it personally

It hurts not to get a job you've taken time and trouble to apply for. But it helps if you keep the following realities in mind.

Recruiters today are usually faced with vast numbers of applications for each job. They usually have limited time and resources to process those applications. Most work hard to do a good job for both employers and candidates but numbers mean decisions are often made very crudely. And the first sift may well be done simply by software looking for particular keywords. That means it is only too easy for an outstanding candidate to be rejected.

Interview panels make decisions based on what they've read and what they make of you on the day. Sometimes this is supplemented by the results from an assessment centre. They make a subjective judgment about the best fit for the role. Their judgment is about a particular role, at that particular point of time. Sometimes, their judgment is clouded by all kinds of factors about which you know nothing. This could include, for example, the internal politics of the organization.

Their decision reflects a view on that particular occasion and it is not about your value as a human being. If they didn't choose you and you were well fitted for the role, they missed out, not just you!

This is an opportunity to learn. Get all the feedback you can from the panel. If they don't offer you an opportunity to discuss your application and the interview, then ask for one. You will find most reputable organizations will have a discussion with you if you have got to interview stage.

Their feedback is valuable. Try not to be defensive. Take a deep breath and listen as objectively as you can to what they have to offer. But weigh their views up for yourself; don't just take it at face value. Do you agree with what they say? What is the evidence?

After your discussion, send a thank you note to whoever took the time-out to give you feedback.

You are not saying thank you out of sheer politeness or gratitude. They may have already offered the job to someone else but that person may change their mind and never start the job. Or the person may take the job but prove to be unsatisfactory.

It happens more often than you think. Filling a job takes an employer a lot of time and energy. Your follow-up discussion, plus your thank you note, will mark you out. It will remind them of you, particularly if you include a request that they get in touch with you if the situation changes or another job becomes available.

Take some time out to reflect positively on the experience you have been through and what you have learned from it. You can't change what has gone before, but you can make sure that your reaction turns into three steps forward and not one step back.

Sometimes things just happen. Now it is time to move on!

The checklist for making a perfect start in your new organization

Congratulations you are about to start your new job.

What can you do to make sure things turn out well?

Here is a checklist for making a perfect start

➡ On your first day, prepare as you did for the interview.

➡ Get a good night's sleep beforehand.

➡ Wear smart, clean and appropriate clothing (check with HR if you are not sure of the dress code).

➡ Make sure you know how to get there and arrive in good time.

➡ Try to make sure you have a contact name.

➡ Once there, learn the culture of your new organization as quickly as you can. Make sure you find out quickly how things get done. Every organization has its own particular style. Watch and listen to find out what it is and how your personality and approach might fit in best.

➡ Get to know who counts in your new workplace. Who are the key decision makers? Make sure you know who needs to be kept on board.

➡ Make sure you have a copy of the job spec and work out for yourself some short term objectives and then work towards them. In due course, make sure you agree the overall objectives for your role with your new boss.

➡ Build up your connections and a new network of contacts, for example colleagues, suppliers and customers, both within the organization and outside it.

➡ Once established, explore the training and experience opportunities and make sure that you understand how appraisals are carried out. Does your organization have a career development program that you can join?

➡ Continue to nurture your network of contacts. Remember networks depend on reciprocity – what do you have to offer others? Think about how you can consolidate your position, make a contribution and then don't wait till it is time to prepare for a move to think about what might come next.

I wish you every success. You can help assure your success by taking advantage of the special offer over the page!

The end?

10% Discount on the Wisewolf Coaching job interview program

Got a job interview coming up? Want to perform at your best?

So, now you know how to set about searching for your job! But putting it all into practice can be daunting. I would like to help and we have a special offer for you.

Two special Job Interview Coaching sessions are available as a package at a reduced price for readers of The WiseWolf Job Search Pocket Book: How to Win Jobs and Influence Recruiters

Find out more at the WiseWolf Coaching website:

http://wisewolfcoaching.com/the-wisewolf-job-search-pocket-book-special-offer/

Use this password to gain access to your page

jobsearchpocketbook

ABOUT THE AUTHOR

Wendy Mason is a qualified and vastly experienced career coach who incorporates life coaching skills to develop her clients' confidence.

As well as being a qualified coach, she is a member of the Association for Coaching and The Institute of Consulting. Wendy holds an advanced diploma in life coaching and a graduate certificate in confidence coaching. She became a coach after a successful career that included work in both the public and private sectors. After gaining a nursing qualification and working as a nurse, she worked as a manager including spells in HR and program management specializing in managing change. She has with organizations as diverse as The Cabinet Office, The BBC and Johnson Controls.

Wendy lives in London with partner Owen. She describes herself as a compulsive blogger (http://wisewolftalking.com). She is a poet and has so far written two novels but has plans for more.

You can contact Wendy at wendymason@wisewolfcoaching.com or follow her on Twitter as @WWisewolf

Printed in Great Britain
by Amazon.co.uk, Ltd.,
Marston Gate.